WRITE YOUR BOOK

7 Steps and 7 Secrets
for Finishing Your Nonfiction Book
Sooner Rather than Later

PETE NIKOLAI
WITH AMELIA NIKOLAI

WESTBOW·
PRESS
A DIVISION OF THOMAS NELSON
& ZONDERVAN

WestBow Press books may be ordered through booksellers or by contacting:

WestBow Press
A Division of Thomas Nelson & Zondervan
1663 Liberty Drive
Bloomington, IN 47403
www.westbowpress.com
1 (866) 928-1240

Because of the dynamic nature of the Internet, any web addresses or
links contained in this book may have changed since publication and
may no longer be valid. The views expressed in this work are solely those
of the author and do not necessarily reflect the views of the publisher,
and the publisher hereby disclaims any responsibility for them.

Certain stock imagery © Thinkstock.
Any people depicted in stock imagery provided by Thinkstock are
models, and such images are being used for illustrative purposes only.

ISBN: 978-1-4908-2838-1 (e)
ISBN: 978-1-4908-2836-7 (sc)

Library of Congress Control Number: 2014907172

Printed in the United States of America.

WestBow Press rev. date: 5/20/2014

For more information on how to write, publish, and market your book, please visit our blog at www.PeteNikolai.com and subscribe.

CONTENTS

PREFACE

IS THIS BOOK FOR YOU?

I n my day job in book publishing, I (Pete) regularly hear from
authors who are struggling to finish their books—and many
who can't even seem to get started. Most authors want to write
faster, and all authors need to write better. If you need to know
how to quickly write a high quality nonfiction book that provides
helpful information to your readers, then this book is for you.

As I have coached authors over the years, I have found that
using this simple writing process improves both the speed and
the quality of the writing. This book will help you determine
how much time you can dedicate to your writing and how to
estimate when each of the drafts in the three draft process will be
finished. While it won't write your book for you, it will provide
an understanding of your productivity and a clear step-by-step
process for finishing your book.

In developing this book, the source materials included my 20+
years of experience in publishing along with the best books on
writing (see bibliography). Our goal has been to condense that

source material so that only the best ideas on the topic remain. Some of the newest books had no new or original information to offer, but they serve as good examples of how aspiring authors are flooding the market with short, practical books.

We won't waste time with stories or amusing anecdotes. You have a book to write and every minute spent doing anything else is a minute that could have been used to finish your book. Let's get it done!

PART ONE

WHY YOU HAVEN'T FINISHED YOUR BOOK— AND WHY YOU WILL

Many writers who struggle to start or finish their books are simply being rational human beings. Writing is something they want to do but so is watching television, catching up with friends online, exercising, pursuing a meaningful relationship, and any number of other worthwhile activities. Writing is difficult and does not provide much immediate gratification. Without sufficient motivation, it just doesn't make sense to invest much time in writing.

For others, perfectionism can cause us to doubt our abilities and to fear doing anything that might not measure up to our own standards or those of others. We fear being recognized as the flawed human beings that we all are (imposter syndrome), and so we avoid taking chances. In doing so, we merely exist until we don't, we accomplish little of significance, and we leave little behind.

To move from safety to significance requires an awakening to the truth, the desire to truly live, the belief that significance is possible, decisive action, and a commitment to persevere no matter the cost. It helps to recognize that everybody lives in fear of not being enough: smart enough, strong enough, good looking enough... We are not responsible for being enough; we are responsible for using what we have to be significant.

Think of the books you have read that helped you in some way. They were written by ordinary people who expressed what they had to say from their unique perspective. No one else could write those books, and no one else can write your book.

We each have today and a limited number of days in the future to do something significant. It is time to find the joy of a life well lived. Following are a few paradigm shifts that help:

- acknowledging that we are all flawed humans
- accepting that some people are not going to like or agree with what you do
- believing that it is okay to fail as long as you learn, persevere, and start again
- appreciating the gifts that God has given you and sharing them with others

For many people, a dream of what life might be like as an author provides the initial inspiration for wanting to write. However it takes more than a dream to get most people to take action. We find the motivation to do hard things by developing perspective, assigning value to things, and believing that the value gained from hard things is better than the value gained from other options. While dreams are nice, they tend to be ephemeral and forgotten rather quickly.

The first of the seven secrets to finishing your book sooner rather than later is to transform your dreams and intentions into your vision so you can determine if you need to write your book and why.

Your vision for what life could be like after you finish your book can inspire you to take action and provide the motivation to persevere and overcome obstacles. To maximize the impact such a vision can have, it helps to capture it in detail using present tense verbs as if you are already there. For example, "I am an author. I regularly receive messages from people who have found help in my book…"

What has been holding you back from writing your book?

_____

_____

_____

_____

What is your vision for what your life could be like after you write your book?

_____

_____

_____

_____

What could writing your book help you to do?

_____

_____

_____

_____

Throughout this book you will find questions like the ones above that are intended to spur your response. You can write your answers in this book (if you have a printed edition), or use a notepad, journal, laptop, tablet, smartphone, or some index cards. Take some time to answer each question. Feel free to repeat yourself as you answer different questions and don't spend too much time editing your answers—you have a book to write.

If you prefer to capture your thoughts digitally then you can find a document listing all the questions at www.PeteNikolai.com/writeyourbook

Each of us has unique purposes for our life and shares common purposes with others. These usually are related to our roles and relationships with other people—what we feel we should accomplish as a parent, spouse, employee, citizen, etc. Others flow from our beliefs about who we are, what we believe our talents and abilities are, and what we believe we exist to be and achieve. Some people believe they understand their purposes very clearly, while others find their understanding evolving over time. Since you are investing your time in completing this book, one of your purposes probably involves writing a book to impact other people.

Authors impact their readers in a variety of ways including the following:

- By providing helpful information
- By explaining complicated topics
- By motivating them to take action
- By enabling them to do something
- By influencing them to consider another perspective

- By persuading them to adopt a different opinion
- By entertaining them with stories

What are your unique purposes currently?

_____

_____

_____

_____

What common purposes do you share with other people?

_____

_____

_____

_____

How do you hope to impact your family, friends, and other people with your writing?

_____

_____

_____

_____

Now that you have captured your purposes and your vision for what life could be like as an author, you have the opportunity to see how your life currently aligns with them. While this can be a rather sobering exercise, it helps to keep in mind that life is a journey, and we do not always have the freedom or resources to do exactly what we want.

How are you currently spending your time—what do you usually do with the 168 hours you have each week (create categories such as sleeping, eating, writing, etc. and determine how many hours you usually spend each week)?

_____

_____

_____

_____

_____

_____

_____

_____

Now go back and rank each category from 0=worthless to 10=most important based on how important each of those activities are to you.

What low importance activities can you cut back on or eliminate and how will you allocate those hours to important activities?

_____

_____

_____

_____

Now go back and list how many hours you would spend on each activity during an ideal week.

What needs to change to make your ideal week more likely?

_____

_____

_____

_____

Similar to a journey, getting from where you are to where you have envisioned requires planning and action. Just as good travel planning can cut down on the time and inconvenience required—and make the trip more enjoyable—so planning your writing can get you where you want to go quicker while helping you avoid bad experiences along the way. A major part of your planning is to establish recognizable milestones for your journey.

The second of the seven secrets to finishing your book sooner rather than later is to capture your goals in writing so you know what you are trying to accomplish.

Keeping your purposes and vision in mind as your destination will help prevent setting goals that take you down the wrong road. When you are capturing your goals, it may be helpful to also capture why completing each goal is important—how it brings you closer to your purposes and vision or helps you avoid roadblocks that might slow you down on your journey. Begin each goal with a verb (create, write, etc.), include an expected completion date to create a sense of urgency, and confirm each goal is measurable so you will know when you have completed it.

As you capture your goals, avoid thinking about all the tactical action steps you might need to take to accomplish a goal so you can avoid getting bogged down in the details. Capture your goals first so you can avoid thinking about and doing stuff that isn't even necessary.

Examples of goals that move you toward the vision of becoming an author include:

- create proposal for <title> by <date>
- write manuscript by <date>
- partner with agent by <date>
- sign with publisher by <date>
- publish book by <date>

Adding expected completion dates helps establish your commitment, provides perspective, and initiates action. Missing a completion date is not failure. It is simply a detour on your journey—an opportunity to evaluate your progress, determine the new best route for getting there based on the additional information available to you, and establish a new expected completion date.

Reviewing your purposes and vision (monthly) and your goals (daily) keeps you focused and headed in the direction you have chosen. It also provides a sense of urgency as you strive to accomplish each goal on time and gives you the opportunity to change course if you realize you need to alter your destination. Reminding yourself of your goals and believing they are important to you and to those you are trying to impact provides the motivation to take the next action step.

Your commitment to achieving your goals enables you to develop an attitude that makes perseverance possible and leads to the highest quality product. Neglecting to remember (aka forgetting) why your goals are important can lead to procrastination and delays.

With your purposes and your vision for your life as an author in mind as your destination, what are the next few major goals you need to achieve to move in the right direction?

_____

_____

_____

_____

_____

Now go back and confirm that you have assigned an expected completion date to each of your goals.

When and where will you review your purposes and vision (monthly) and your goals (daily)?

_____

_____

_____

_____

_____

Once you have identified your goals, it is much easier to see what is necessary to accomplish them. The difference between those who have goals and those who achieve them usually comes down to listing the sequence of action steps that must be taken. Once you have listed the action steps then accomplishing the goal is as easy as completing each step.

Any time you are doing stuff that is not an action step toward accomplishing one of your goals you are either wasting time, procrastinating, or working on somebody else's goals. Doing stuff as directed by your employer is necessary and probably should be thought of as an action step toward accomplishing your goals if the income is needed to give you the opportunity to pursue your vision. Doing stuff to help your friends and family accomplish their goals is also necessary, but you have to be careful to find the appropriate balance between helping others and pursuing your vision. Helping others also makes them more likely to help you, and healthy interdependency expedites the accomplishment of many goals since you can draw from others' strengths in areas where you are weak.

Listing the action steps also helps clarify which goals might be more difficult to achieve than others. If you struggle to determine a sequence of action steps to accomplish a goal then it may be necessary to break down a goal into several goals, learn more about what is necessary to accomplish a goal, or acknowledge there is no clear set of action steps you can take to accomplish a particular goal because some of the steps are out of your control or even unknown.

The third of the seven secrets to finishing your book sooner rather than later is to list the action steps necessary to accomplish each goal so you know what needs to be done and what to do next.

Similar to goals, each action step should start with a verb (create, write, etc.) and be measurable so you know when you have completed it. If an action step seems too difficult then break it down further so you can move closer to your goal by completing some step. The intention to "write a book" someday takes on urgency when it becomes the goal to "write manuscript by <date>" that then becomes possible when broken down into an achievable "write 300 words" recurring action step.

Hitting the New York Times Best Seller List is a goal that depends on action steps that are unknown or out of the control of most authors. This reality does not mean you should not have the goal, it just means you've identified a difficult goal you will return to over time as you gain understanding of what action steps might be necessary or when factors outside your control come together to accomplish something you could not. If you do not have any difficult goals for which you are struggling to identify all the action steps then you may not be pushing yourself to accomplish all you could. Identifying and striving to achieve difficult goals takes character, perseverance, and the ability to ask for help. It involves risk and uncomfortable interdependence, but it leads to a life of significance and meaning.

What are the action steps for each of the goals you have identified?

_____

_____

_____

_____

_____

What difficult goals have you identified (those for which you can't currently list a sequence of achievable action steps to accomplish)?

_____

_____

_____

_____

_____

PART TWO

GETTING IT DONE

Writing probably isn't as easy for you as making breakfast or getting ready for work—at least not yet. Professional writers (those who generate their income from writing) usually do most of their writing on the job during work hours at their office. You will have to go about it differently.

Most authors write their first book either early in the morning or late at night. Jot down your schedule for each day of the week: when do you get up, leave for work, get home, get to bed? Determine when you can make time for writing each day of the week and how much time you can add. I (Pete) found I could get up an hour and a half earlier Monday through Friday, two and a half hours earlier on Saturday, and also write for two hours on Sunday evenings so I found twelve hours per week I have blocked off as my writing time.

I did not feel like getting up earlier, but I made a decision to be an author and to embrace everything that comes with the job.

Choosing to be an author is choosing to take a second job. As with any job, there are expectations and requirements. Performing well requires showing up on time, learning on the job, choosing to maintain a thankful attitude, and doing your best.

The fourth of the seven secrets to finishing your book sooner rather than later is to identify as much time as possible during your week for writing and to reserve those times by scheduling writing appointments on your calendar.

Many writers find the first half hour of each session is the least productive, so a one hour session only has 30 minutes of maximum productivity, and longer sessions are more productive so try to schedule at least 90 minutes per appointment. As much as possible, schedule your writing appointments during the time of day when you are most productive and creative. Treat them as some of the most important time on your calendar each week.

Assign a location to your writing appointments. Find or create an environment that helps you minimize interruptions and maximize your output. For many writers this means finding a place that is relatively free of distractions. Some do better with quiet, others with music, and others with background white noise that can be tuned out.

What time of day are you most productive and creative?

When will you write throughout the week?

_____

_____

_____

How many hours per week have you scheduled for writing?

_____

_____

_____

Where do you think you will be most productive when writing?

_____

_____

_____

Choosing to be an author also involves adopting certain perspectives and attitudes. By writing a book you are declaring to the world that you are an authority on your topic so be an authority! Write about a topic you understand thoroughly but make sure you focus on helping readers with a narrow specific need. Readers are leery of broad, high page count, high priced books by new authors. If you want to address more than one need then write more than one book.

James Hall's book *Hit Lit: Cracking the Code of the 20th Century's Biggest Bestsellers* attempts to do what publishers and authors have failed to do since Gutenberg: identify what determines whether or not a book will become a bestseller. While *Hit Lit* focuses on novels, much of what he attempts to do should go into every author's thinking as they determine what to write, how to write it, and how to get readers to buy it:

1. Identify what readers want and need. Bestsellers tend to include similar themes and elements that appeal to common wants and needs. We are fascinated by stories of fractured families, spiritual quests, doubts resolved, and common sense overcoming shrewd manipulation. We want to learn something along the way and even gain an understanding of current issues. We try to be like people who take risks and act decisively as they work through conflicts and dilemmas.

2. Write well. As editor Michael Korda said, "At least half the books on any given week's bestseller list are there to the immense surprise and puzzlement of their publishers." If a book triggers an emotional response in readers that causes them to mention the book to others then the fire has fuel. Many bestsellers deal with common wants and needs in new ways. While there is "nothing new under the sun" there are new ways of saying things.

3. Get readers excited. While publishers and authors with connections to millions of readers have a distinct advantage, they really do not have absolute power to drive sales of an inferior book. More important is getting the book in the hands and minds of influential individuals and communities of readers who would have a natural affinity

for the book. If they get excited about it then they will pour more fuel on the fire.

4. Get lucky/blessed. It is easy to find books very similar to any bestseller. Some are better written. Some were released before the bestseller and some after. What caused one to ignite while the others fizzled? A lit match dropped on a pile of dry tinder has a much better chance of igniting a fire than one dropped on soggy logs. A book with a new approach to address a common need that is in the spotlight just when the urgency of that need increases for some reason can catch fire.

5. Repeat. The good news for successful authors is that readers who like a book usually want more from the same author. We all have limited time and resources so we prefer to use brands we trust.

Since much of what determines whether a book sells well or not can't be controlled or even influenced by an author, it makes sense to focus on the things that can be impacted. Write from your unique experience to provide a unique perspective. Even if you are writing on a topic that has been covered extensively, creating a unique book addressing a specific need in a new way can enable you to make a difference in the lives of your readers.

As you have read books, articles, and blog posts on your topic you probably found yourself disagreeing with key points. Focus your writing on your unique perspective and where your thinking is different from others so you address the topic in a new way and add value. Draw from your unique life experiences (successes and mistakes) and expertise to create a book that will strike a chord where the current material only seems to be worthless noise.

Analyze similar books on the topic (aka category) on Amazon to see how much demand there is, which ones are most popular, and what features or benefits might be causing them to be more popular.

What specific need do you want to help readers with?

_____

_____

_____

What is lacking in current books on the topic and how will your book be different?

_____

_____

_____

How will your reader's life be different after reading your book?

_____

_____

_____

Accept responsibility for who you are, for what you have experienced, and for what you will experience in the days to come—because you are responsible. Accepting responsibility does not mean taking the blame or punishing yourself for your mistakes. It means choosing to understand what has happened, learning from it, determining what you will do if you face a similar situation in the future, and perhaps even helping others experience similar successes or avoid similar mistakes.

Which life experiences do you want to share and what did you learn from each?

_____

_____

_____

_____

_____

_____

Accepting responsibility also involves choosing to have an attitude that is neither proud nor self-defeating, but is humble, thankful, open to learning, and ready to persevere and make the most of each moment. It requires that you tell yourself (and others if appropriate) the truth about what has happened rather than living in denial or fear while lying to yourself and others. We each have an ongoing commentary in our thoughts and can choose what we tell ourselves. We can choose to create stories that hold us back and build hurdles that make success more difficult, or we can choose to believe things that help us adjust quickly and maintain a good attitude.

Again, this does not mean beating yourself up but instead putting things in perspective to avoid making too much of your successes and mistakes so you can focus on what you have learned, be thankful for each experience, understand what you should do in the moment you are currently living, and choose to do it. Authors with a thankful attitude tend to experience more success since publishers and others in the industry prefer to work with them rather than those who are proud and self-serving.

Accepting responsibility is one of the first steps in preparing and planning for the future. Being prepared involves knowing yourself, believing in your abilities, and believing your actions are worth taking. Journaling can be helpful in getting your thoughts out where you can see them clearly and work through them. One way to capture your beliefs is to write each one as an affirmation to recite on a regular basis when you are alone. Doing so can help you counter the tendency to forget those beliefs or minimize their importance. Following are some examples:

- what I have to say is important and will make a difference
- if the reader will put these ideas into practice then their life will be transformed
- helping others gives meaning and purpose to my life

What is the truth about what you have experienced?

_____

_____

_____

What do you want to help others learn from your experiences?

_____

_____

_____

What do you believe about yourself and your writing that you want to affirm regularly?

_____

_____

_____

```
STEP      CREATING YOUR
  2       BOOK PROPOSAL
```

As you are preparing to write or continue writing your book, think like a builder. Whether you are writing a book or building a house, work with the potential buyers in mind—what they want and value. If a buyer is looking for a four bedroom house for their family with three kids and the builder is trying to sell a two bedroom condo then it will do the builder little good to focus on how wonderful it is to be able to avoid mowing a yard. However if the buyer is single and likes the idea of not having a yard to maintain then they are probably in the market for a condo.

Just as a builder does a careful study of the wants and needs of a particular neighborhood before determining what kind of house to build and then draws up a house plan to meet those specifications, so an author should carefully study and document the wants and needs of their target market and then create a plan to guide their writing. You don't want to finish your book only to find out there is little need for it or that three other books by well-known authors are available with a very similar message.

The fifth of the seven secrets to finishing your book sooner rather than later is to develop your book proposal to determine if there is a market for your book and, if so, to plan your book with your market in mind.

A book proposal serves functions similar to a real estate market analysis, a house plan, and a for-sale listing for a house. Before a builder breaks ground to start construction, they first do a market analysis to determine how strong the market is for the type of house they intend to build and if the competition has saturated the market. If the market is strong and not saturated, then the builder develops the plan for a house their target customer will need and want.

The house plan enables the builder to determine if the house can be built at a cost that will allow it to be sold at a price a buyer will be willing to pay while also allowing the builder to make sufficient profit. Once the builder is confident the house they intend to build is one their target customer will want then they will usually work with their agent to develop a comprehensive for-sale listing and put the house on the market *before they even break ground* so they can contract with the buyer before they incur any additional expense.

If you are a builder then it is not enough to just build a house, you have to build what real estate agents, investors, and potential homeowners want and then sell it. As an author, it is not enough to just write a book, you have to write what readers (and agents and publishers if you want to be traditionally published) want and then sell it.

Regardless of whether you intend to self-publish your book or to try to hire an agent to pursue having it traditionally published, you should go through the steps involved in creating a book proposal before you write another word of the manuscript:

- summarize your book along with its features and benefits
- determine the categories and topic
- determine the trends for those categories and topic (the categories are the broad subjects usually noted in terms of standard BISAC Subject Headings; the topic is usually an author-defined subdivision within those categories and should correspond to a clearly identified area of reader interest)
- identify the strongest competitive titles, determine the strengths and weaknesses of each, and determine how your book stacks up against each
- identify the target market for your book and determine the size of that market
- provide information on what qualifies you to write this book and what you will bring to the table to help the book sell
- determine a preliminary title for your book that clearly communicates what it is about and what makes it unique (this is listed after the previous steps since they help inform your thinking on what the preliminary title should be)
- create a chapter-by-chapter synopsis of what you intend to write

Each of these steps will be explained in detail in the following pages. Capturing your idea in a well-developed book proposal is one of the most important steps in writing your book and will help you clarify if and why your book is needed. In the process you will come to understand who your customer is and why they need to read your book. Your proposal will help you develop a plan for writing your book. It will be used by service providers (editor, cover designer, publicist, etc.) so they can quickly understand what is being created and what is expected. In addition, parts of the proposal are used as the foundation for your book's marketing plan that outlines media appearances, speaking events, product placement, advertising, etc.

Since your proposal is so important, it should be well written just like any good marketing copy:

- Pay attention to formatting. Use bullets to call out important points and paragraphs to add details and description. While authors hope agents and publishers (and book readers) are reading rather than scanning, many are doing a mix of both whether we like it or not. You provide a valuable service when you format your proposal (and book) to align with readers' preferences.

- Use crisp and clear language. Avoiding long sentences and speaking simply help make the information easier to process quickly. Say what your customer needs to read as efficiently as possible. Agents and publishers are looking for authors who demonstrate they can distill information into its most potent form.

- Avoid copywriting mistakes. Covering every important angle, establishing a consistent tone, and avoiding subcultural and regional jargon (such as "Christianese" or "Southern") in your proposal (and book) can go a long way in helping agents and publishers understand what you are trying to say and confirming you have the ability to write an authoritative treatment on your topic.

- Establish trust. Using an editor's help to avoid grammar and spelling mistakes helps establish your credibility. Simplifying your explanations of technical issues so even a novice can understand also helps build trust that readers will appreciate the information you intend to provide.

- Go above and beyond the basics. Finding the optimum mix between writing that is informative, inspiring, simple, creative, and engaging makes the difference between a proposal (and book) that gets started and one that gets read.
- Outrank the competition. If you read several proposals (and books) on the same topic, you'll probably find they all start to sound the same and draw from the same sources. Doing original research or finding the sources others did not bother to dig for can give your proposal (and book) an edge on the competition and more impact on your readers.

To develop your proposal, create a new document and capture the information described below under the following section headings: Premise, Unique Selling Proposition (USP), Categories and Topic, Seasonal Tie-In Opportunities, Life Event Tie-In Opportunities, Competitive Market Analysis, Target Market, Preliminary Title and Subtitle, and Synopsis.

Premise

After the title page, the first section of a book proposal is the premise which is a summary of what your book is about including the problem or need it addresses, the promise of a solution, and a description of how the reader's life will be better—all in 150 words or less. For example, if we were writing a book to help people understand why to invest and how to take advantage of automatic investments, our premise might be something like:

> Financial advisors recommend people have retirement savings of at least twice their annual salary by age 35, three times their salary by age 45, five times by age

55, and seven times by age 65. They also recommend parents have half a year's tuition saved by the time their child is 6, one year's tuition saved by the time they are 12, and two years by the time they are 18. Yet few of us meet any of those standards. This book will help readers understand and appreciate their need to invest. It will provide a simple plan for taking advantage of automatic investment opportunities and motivate readers to take simple action steps. By doing so, readers can maintain or even improve their standard of living year after year, meet their family's needs, and experience the joy and freedom of financial independence.

Unique Selling Proposition

The Unique Selling Proposition (USP) expands on the solution promised in the premise by listing the key takeaways or benefits the reader will obtain due to the features the book provides. It can be stated as follows:

> The reader of this book will <benefits> because the book will <features>.

For our book on automatic investing, the USP might be something like:

> The reader of this book will develop the desire and ability to invest because the book will help them understand how their emotional state will improve when they are prepared for the future, how they will be free to focus on pursuing their dreams rather worrying about their lack of resources, and how automatic investing is simple and easy.

Categories and Topic

In publishing, a book's categories are the broad subjects usually noted in terms of two to three official BISAC Subject Headings. The topic is usually an author-defined subdivision within those categories and should correspond to a clearly identified area of reader interest. It serves to place parameters on the market so it is broad enough to have the potential to generate substantial sales but narrow enough to be marketed to efficiently.

You can find the current list of BISAC Subject Headings at https://www.bisg.org/bisac-subject-codes

For our book on automatic investing, the categories would be:

BUS050020 BUSINESS & ECONOMICS / Personal Finance / Investing

BUS050040 BUSINESS & ECONOMICS / Personal Finance / Retirement Planning

The topic could be stated as: why to invest and how to set up automatic investments

In addition to determining the categories and topic, you should also research the trends in interest in your topic using tools such as Google Trends. When you go to the Google Trends site at http://www.google.com/trends/ you can scroll down to click the "More to Explore" link, add a term such as "investing," select dates to have the data show the last couple of years, and see a chart showing the trend over that time. The URL can then be copied and pasted into your proposal.

The chart on "investing" shows an increase in interest over the past 18 months and a spike in January each year which may indicate that December would be a good month to release our book on investing. A similar chart on your topic showing increasing interest during the past year or two helps confirm your topic may be in demand.

Seasonal Tie-In Opportunities

As we saw with our investing book, many topics have seasonal trends that authors, publishers, and book retailers can take advantage of to increase sales. Many retailers see their highest sales during the Christmas season, but there are several other gift-giving occasions and topical interest spikes throughout the year that provide marketing and merchandising opportunities. Unless your book is Christmas-themed, you will probably be better served by tying your release date and initial promotion to another marketing opportunity so as to avoid getting buried by the avalanche of new products released for the Christmas selling season.

Following are the primary seasonal merchandising themes book retailers use: new year, winter, black history month, Valentine's Day, spring, Easter, Mother's Day, Memorial Day, graduation, summer, Father's Day, Independence Day, back to school, fall, Halloween, election day, Thanksgiving, and Christmas.

Life Event Tie-In Opportunities

In addition to the seasonal tie-in opportunities, many products sell well throughout the year due to their appeal for weddings, anniversaries, birthdays, and other life events.

Competitive Market Analysis

The most eye-opening step in creating your book proposal may be doing your market analysis since it requires that you obtain detailed information on titles that would be competing with your book and gain a sense of the saturation level of the market for your topic.

—— find a book on the same topic on Amazon and scroll down to the "Look for Similar Items by Category" section to see the book's subject categories

—— click the category that seems to most closely match your book to see the current top sellers in that category

—— *What are five titles that seem to be very similar to your book?*

_____   _____

_____   _____

_____   _____

_____   _____

_____   _____

_____   _____

_____   _____

_____   _____

— scroll down to the "Product Details" section on the page for one of those books and click a different category to see the current top sellers in that category

— add a few more titles to your list of similar books

— repeat until you feel you have identified 15-20 of the most competitive books

— use your judgment to determine the top five competitors for your book and fill out a Competitive Analysis Form on each of them (this form is available for download at www.PeteNikolai.com/writeyourbook so you can quickly select the data on Amazon, copy it, and paste it as text on the form)

Competitive Analysis Form

Complete this form for each competitive title.

Title: Click here to enter text.

Author: Click here to enter text.

Paperback

List Price: Click here to enter text.

Current Amazon New Price: Click here to enter text.

Lowest Used Price: Click here to enter text.

You can either manually populate the following data, or copy the Product Details section off Amazon paste it over the following Page Count through Category Ranks headings:

Page Count:

Publisher:

Date Published:

ISBN-10:

ISBN-13:

Product Dimensions:

Average Customer Review and Number of Reviews:

Amazon Best Sellers Rank:

Category Ranks:

Hardcover

List Price: Click here to enter text.

Current Amazon New Price: Click here to enter text.

Lowest Used Price: Click here to enter text.

You can either manually populate the following data, or copy the Product Details section off Amazon paste it over the following Page Count through Category Ranks headings:

Page Count:

When you have filled out a Competitive Analysis Form on each of the top five competitive books, review the information to determine if the market for books on your topic seems to be saturated. If the bestselling books on the topic have strong reviews and were published in the past couple of years then the market for books on that topic is more saturated (and harder to break into) than if the bestselling books on the topic have weak reviews or were published several years ago.

If none of the bestselling books on the topic have a Best Sellers Rank (sales rank when compared to all books sold on Amazon) in the top 20,000 then the topic is not currently in high demand and the potential sales level is relatively low.

Evaluating the saturation level and potential sales level is subjective. There is always room for a definitive book that includes new information readers want and need, but your competitive analysis will give you a better understanding of how receptive the market will likely be toward your proposed book, and it demonstrates to potential agents and prospective publishers that you understand the market.

Search the internet for articles, blog posts, and other content sources providing a comprehensive and high quality discussion of your topic since many people will be unlikely to buy a book if they can obtain the information for free. The content you find online should also be considered as source material for your book.

Examining the competitive books, articles, and blog posts should provide some perspective on whether the scope of what you have in mind is sufficient to require a book or would be better served by an article or blog post. Doing so also helps determine whether or not the information you intend to provide is unique enough to deliver sufficient value to cause your target readers to be willing to purchase your book. If not, then either figure out how to add more value, switch to a topic on which you can deliver sufficient value, or be satisfied with self-publishing a book that will likely have modest retail sales at best.

Jumping on a bandwagon (e.g., heaven books) at the same time as several well-known authors can inhibit your book's sales, but identifying a trend or cultural tie-in opportunity early and being one of the first with a high-quality book capitalizing on a spike in interest increases your chances of establishing yourself as a leading voice and of obtaining publicity.

If you decide to try to have your book traditionally published, then the publishers of competitive books are usually the best prospects since publishers prefer to have several titles in the same category to market together, and editors and other team members tend to develop category expertise that should be helpful as they work on your book. Having said that, do not spend much time at this point figuring out the world of book publishing—too many authors allow learning about publishing to become a major distraction that keeps them from finishing their book.

Publishers and agents will only consider new authors who have finished a strong manuscript unless the author is communicating regularly with hundreds of thousands of followers. The purpose of creating a proposal at this stage is to confirm whether your book idea is viable and to provide perspective on the market that will help as you write your book.

Once you complete your market analysis, answer these questions:

Is the market saturated with recent high-quality competitive products?

_____

Is the topic currently in high demand?

_____

Can you add new information and a valuable perspective on the topic?

_____

How will your book deliver more value than the current top titles on the topic so prospective readers will choose your book?

_____

_____

_____

_____

Is the topic covered well in the free content available online?

_____

What should be included in your manuscript for it to have a broad enough scope to justify a book rather than a blog post or magazine article?

_____

_____

_____

Have other authors on the topic established competitive barriers with their brands, platforms, and networks?

_____

Are there any trends or cultural tie-in opportunities spiking interest in the topic?

_____

_____

_____

Should you write the book you are proposing? If not, have you identified some ideas for potentially better opportunities?

_____

_____

Target Market

Many authors tend to think readers know what they want and are buying based on those preferences, and so we tend to imitate bestselling books in hopes of giving readers what they want. We need to realize readers are simply choosing the best available option. They don't really know what else they might want because they can't imagine it. Some may be able to imagine it but find it difficult to put into words. How do you describe something that doesn't exist? Or how do you find the courage to admit you want something nobody else is saying they want? As Steve Jobs said, "people don't know what they want until you show it to them."

Rather than trying to create the perfect book everybody needs, we should realize there are many great books but not one that meets the needs of everybody. We have the opportunity to create books that meet the needs of large segments of the population who only read books that are not normal—books that don't show up on bestseller lists. By doing so, we increase the average level of satisfaction with our writing dramatically, as we write from our unique perspective in our unique style for people with unique needs and desires. We can't please everybody, but we can be successful if we focus on pleasing somebody.

As you are determining who it is you expect to purchase your book and why, think in terms of their demographic characteristics and their motivations or felt needs. While you may think the market for your book is every person who can read, you (or perhaps your publisher) will not have a marketing budget to target the world so be specific as to the market most likely to purchase your book and the affinity groups within that market.

Your description of the market for your book should be 50 words or less and can include their gender, age, education attained, geographic location, socio-economic status, religious preference, political inclination, occupation, hobbies, values, motivations, wants, needs, goals, seasonal purchasing needs, fears, frustrations, problems, etc. Strike a balance between narrowing the market to make it easy to target and identifying a large market so you (and perhaps your publisher) can envision high sales and justify a substantial marketing budget to drive those sales. You can even choose to personify your market by creating customer personas with nicknames that include an attribute.

For our book on automatic investing, the description of the market might be something like:

The market includes:

- Confused Charlie and Bewildered Barb: people aged 18–40 who realize they need to invest but are uncertain or confused about investing and want it to be quick and easy
- Generous Jerry and Loving Louise: people who want to give a practical book as a gift

Who are the customers for your book (the market) and how would you describe them?

_____

_____

_____

_____

The people in your target market will usually tend to exhibit similar behaviors and either formally or informally belong to affinity groups that can make marketing to them easier. They subscribe to the same newsletters, listen to the same podcasts, visit the same websites, belong to the same organizations, attend the same meetings, utilize the same services, purchase products from the same companies, etc. By listing those affinity groups, you (and perhaps any prospective agents and publishers) can catch a vision for how easy it will be to market your book to your target market.

Just as you don't want the target market to be too broad, you also don't want it to be too fragmented. Take a few minutes to brainstorm as many affinity groups as possible, but then choose the top three. Hopefully there will be many people outside your target market who will also buy your book, but having a specific market and affinity groups in mind guides your sales and marketing efforts. It also helps to have affinity groups identified before you begin your manuscript so you can develop your topic and write with them in mind.

Following are a few affinity groups for our book on automatic investing:

- new parents (interested in saving for college)
- new employees (need insight on retirement saving plans they are eligible to join)
- parents of new parents and new employees (want to give a practical gift)

What are the top three affinity groups for your book?

_____

_____

_____

Preliminary Title and Subtitle

At this stage, you just want a preliminary title and subtitle that clearly communicate what your book will be about. Don't try to be overly creative or spend too much time—you need a placeholder to capture the key benefit you want to provide and help guide your writing.

For our book on automatic investing, the preliminary title and subtitle could be something like *Automatic Investing: The Quick and Easy Way to Prepare for the Future and Support Pursuing Your Dreams.*

What is your preliminary title and subtitle?

_____

_____

About the Author

Agents, publishers, and readers value the expertise of an author who has been successful doing what their book advocates in the real world. In the case of our book on automatic investing, an author that has done substantial research on the topic, has credentials as a financial advisor with several years of experience helping others grow their investments, and has been successful in growing their own investments will probably be seen as qualified to write the book.

However, there is a big difference between having expertise and being ready to become a successful author. That difference is found in the other five elements that agents and traditional publishers are looking to acquire:

- your writing ability
- your established brand that positions you as a well-known and respected authority on the topic in the market
- your established platform that enables you to communicate with your audience as needed and to spur them into action
- your sizable audience that looks to you for advice and will buy your book (and perhaps even similar books on an affiliate basis)
- your established network that is ready, willing, and able to use their platforms and communicate with their audiences to help make the market aware of your book and drive sales

Agents and publishers want to see previously published work that is well written, widely read, and well received. Our financial writer should have previous books that have sold well or several recent articles or blog posts on popular financial or general interest websites that have received positive comments. Even better, they should have a regular column on one or more sites, a radio show or podcast, and their own blog with a substantial number of unique visitors each month.

Publishing is a business. As mentioned previously, agents and publishers have an abundance of proposals from which to choose so they are going to choose the ones that seem likely to deliver the highest profits with the lowest risk and least work. While "the squeaky wheel gets the grease" it is also true that the wheel that keeps squeaking gets replaced—nobody wants to work with somebody who is demanding, self-centered, and constantly complaining.

Freelance publicists, media producers and hosts, editors, marketers, and everybody else in the industry will want to work with a professional author that writes well, has ideas and content that meets the needs of a large market, has an established and respected brand, has a platform that reaches a sizable audience that will purchase a substantial number of copies, has a network of connections to help make the market aware of each new book, is low maintenance, is a pleasure to do business with, helps them be successful, and focuses their books on helping others.

What education, experience, and expertise do you have that qualifies you to write the book?

_____

_____

_____

How have you demonstrated that you have the ability to write content that people find interesting and valuable?

_____

_____

_____

What brand have you built that establishes you as a respected authority on the topic in the market?

_____

_____

_____

_____

What platform have you built that will enable you to communicate with your audience and help market the book?

_____

_____

_____

_____

What audience have you developed that you can communicate with as needed?

_____

_____

_____

_____

What network have you established that will enable you to make the market aware of your book?

Synopsis

Once you've established there is a need for your book, identified the market and the top affinity groups, and determined your preliminary title and subtitle, then you are ready to start capturing your ideas and providing some structure to your book. Before you can outline the content to be contained in your manuscript, you need to have a good idea of the various concepts and ideas it could potentially include.

As you have been researching and thinking about your topic on and off for some time, your mind has been generating related concepts and ideas based on your experience and knowledge. Now is the time to capture as many of those thoughts and questions as possible so you can see the material you have available to build your synopsis. Use brainstorming to quickly capture everything that comes to mind related to your topic and target market without editing or judging. Purge your mind for at least 30 minutes. Feel free to write on a flip chart, index cards, a notepad—whatever allows you to capture everything quickly without pausing to organize or edit.

When you are finished, organize those concepts and ideas to outline a chapter-by-chapter synopsis detailing what you intend to cover. Group similar thoughts together and develop 7-14 preliminary chapter titles and 2-3 bullet points per chapter describing the key takeaways or action items your target market will find important. Doing so causes you to think your book through to the end and prepares you to write the manuscript.

What are all your concepts, ideas, and questions about your topic? Capture on a flip chart, index cards, a notepad, etc.

What is the synopsis for your book? Capture on a flip chart, index cards, a notepad, etc.

In the process of completing your proposal, you determined if writing the book makes sense and captured your ideas for what content to include. Next you will determine the schedule for completing your first draft and create a detailed plan for writing your book.

| STEP 3 | DETERMINING YOUR DEADLINE AND HOW YOU WILL MEET IT |

Writing a book is like hiking the Appalachian Trail. It seems like you're travelling quickly at first as you leave your starting terminus behind. However, after you've been on the trail for a few days, it can seem like you're barely moving and will never reach your destination. So you start to wonder if you should just give up and go back.

But thru-hikers starting with a thorough understanding of what to expect including how long the trip will take can choose to press on in spite of their perceptions. If they know the trail is 2,200 miles and that they average 22 miles per day then they know they will reach their destination in approximately 100 days—and so they can choose to keep hiking. Their goal changes from hiking an overwhelming 2,200 miles to a series of recurring goals to simply enjoy a hike on the trail today. In the same way, if you know you need to write a first draft of 20,000 words and that you average 500 words per hour then you can choose to keep writing to get to the 40 hours needed. You can change an overwhelming goal into a series of achievable recurring goals to simply show up and write today.

To establish your perspective on how you will finish your first draft, determine how many words it should be and how many words you average per hour of writing. Books in general seem to be getting shorter as readers' preferences adjust to the way they spend their time. Many popular topical books that are intended to be sold primarily as an ebook are just 10,000-15,000 words, but popular nonfiction books in bookstores tend to average 30,000 words or more. Writers vary widely in their productivity, but most average 500-1,500 words per hour when writing a first draft. If you don't know how many words per hour you normally write, use 500 as a preliminary estimate and update it based on your actual productivity after a week or two of writing.

What is your preliminary expected word count for your book?

_____

What is your preliminary expected writing productivity per hour?

_____

Using your answers to those questions and the earlier question of how many hours per week you have scheduled to write, it is relatively simple to estimate the date when you could finish writing your first draft. Subtract the number of words you have written so far (found in the bottom left corner of the screen if you are using Microsoft Word) from your expected word count, divide that number by your expected words per hour, divide the result by the number of hours per week you have scheduled to write, and you have calculated a preliminary estimate for how many weeks you need to finish your first draft. Look at your calendar, count that many weeks into the future, and add a "celebrate finishing first draft" appointment on that Friday or Saturday.

What is your expected completion date for your first draft?

Now you have a deadline to meet—and that's a good thing. The absence of deadlines and appointments contributes to a writer watching TV or browsing the internet rather than working on their manuscript and becoming a better writer. A writer without deadlines and appointments is usually a writer who is easily distracted. Once you have scheduled your writing appointments and established your deadline, you have a milestone that comes with opportunities and responsibilities. Success comes from embracing those opportunities and responsibilities each day and finding joy in the new stage of life you have entered. You are now an author writing your book.

Motivation and inspiration can also be found by reminding yourself why it is important to write your book. You answered questions earlier to help you develop the perspective and attitude of an author. Schedule a monthly appointment to review and update your answers to those questions.

While it is nearly impossible to write a book today, it can be wonderful to have the opportunity and responsibility to produce 300 or 600 or 1,000 words today, and tomorrow, and the next day... Some days are much more difficult than others, so give yourself mercy and grace by accepting the 200 word days as necessary steps toward the 1,500 word days.

While you are investing your time in writing each day, there are several things you can do to increase your output so you might even finish your first draft ahead of schedule. For many aspiring authors, the biggest roadblock to finishing their book is the amount of time they spend doing other things, whether consciously choosing to do so or not.

The sixth of the seven secrets to finishing your book sooner rather than later is replacing the time you spend doing less important things with writing time by scheduling even more writing appointments on your calendar.

Doing so will have to come at the expense of other priorities, but what is more important to you? Many writers choose to unplug their television and put it in the closet until they write their book—and many then choose to get rid of it completely or to place strict limits on their TV time so they can write another book or accomplish other priorities.

Another important limit to establish is the amount of time you will spend developing your brand, platform, audience, and network (we'll lump these together under "platform development"). While spending time building relationships on your platform is necessary, it is only part of what authors do. Many authors try to write their books incrementally using blogging to obtain immediate feedback. While this can be helpful, it is too easy to become a blogger rather than an author and to eventually realize you are making little progress toward finishing your book. Every hour you spend on social media is an hour you could have invested in writing or editing.

The amount of platform development time necessary fluctuates based on where you are in the writing-publishing-marketing cycle.

Be intentional by scheduling appropriate "platform development" appointments based on the phase you are in currently. Be vigilant to make sure social media is serving your purposes rather than becoming a slave to social media—too many people are wasting large parts of their lives online as they neglect their goals, dreams, relationships, and other priorities.

The number of books, blogs, and conferences on writing is both a blessing and a curse. Too many writers read too much and write too little. Their actions and their spending reveal they are really readers who write a little from time to time. Others spend more time at writers' conferences or posting in online writers forums than writing. While it is important to keep learning throughout life, the ratios of learning-to-doing and learning-to-teaching should change substantially as your formal education ends, your primary source of learning transitions to experience and relationships, and you move into positions of responsibility and authority. With this book's help, you are graduating from the school of writing, getting a job (finishing your book), and getting to work. To spend an appropriate amount of time learning, schedule "author education" appointments and keep them limited.

As you cut back on time spent watching television, browsing the internet, developing your platform, learning about writing, and doing other things, schedule more writing appointments to make sure you use your time to accomplish your priorities.

STEP 4 > CREATING YOUR WRITING PLAN

In addition to increasing the amount of time you invest in writing, you can also take steps to improve your writing productivity. Many authors waste a lot of time. They resemble a traveler who undertakes a journey without a map or any type of navigation device. They may get there eventually, but they will waste a lot of time backtracking and figuring out what to do next.

The last of the seven secrets to finishing your book sooner rather than later is to develop and use a detailed writing plan.

As you created your book proposal, you brainstormed the concepts and ideas to be included in your book and outlined a chapter-by-chapter synopsis with chapter titles and 2-3 bullet points per chapter. Copy and paste that synopsis into a new document and save it as the plan for your book. Then take an hour or two to build out the outline for each chapter by adding more bullet points for the other concepts and ideas from your previous brainstorming plus quick references to the source materials you have found and questions to be answered.

Plan your book with your customer personas in mind: What do they need to read? What problems are you going to help them solve? Imagine them gathered around you to help you develop your plan. They need to know what you know about the topic—they need your help. Write down the questions they would ask and quick bullet-point answers along with other bullet-point information on each subtopic in each chapter.

Plan to start with a chapter discussing your customer's situation, the problems they are dealing with, and how you have the solution. The solution is not easy or obvious, or they would not need your book. End the chapter with a quick explanation of how you were in a similar situation, how you found a solution that improved your situation, and how you will share that solution in the remaining chapters.

Why are your customers stuck?

_____

_____

_____

_____

_____

What questions would they ask?

_____

_____

_____

What questions would they not know to ask?

_____

_____

_____

What did you do differently or what knowledge do you have that allowed you to solve the problem?

_____

_____

_____

Why were you in a position to solve the problem?

_____

_____

_____

Why are you an authority?

_____

_____

_____

As you develop your plan, you may notice gaps in the information and identify questions you can't answer. Make a note of those and schedule a research appointment to obtain that information later so you can stay focused on developing your plan now. Map out your plan from start to finish with as much detail as seems appropriate so you know what you will write and will be able to simply follow your directions rather than trying to figure out what your manuscript should contain while you are trying to write.

Before you begin writing your manuscript, schedule research appointments to complete the research necessary to fill in the gaps and answer the questions you have identified. Add that information to your plan and confirm it is complete and in order so you avoid the speed-bumps that could slow you down when you are writing.

STEP 5 〉 WRITING YOUR FIRST DRAFT

Congratulations! If you are reading this then you should have established your expected completion date for your first draft and completed your writing plan. If not then put this book and all other distractions away, get it done, and come back to this book only when you have established your expected completion date for your first draft and completed your writing plan.

Completing your writing plan is the critical step for most aspiring authors, so you are well on the way to finishing your book. Next up is the writing. You have built out an outline for each chapter with bullet points for the content and concepts your customer personas need to know. Now you get to set your creative mind free to generate the amazing content that will fill the pages of your first draft.

As mentioned previously, many writers find the first half hour of each session is the least productive, so a one hour session only has 30 minutes of maximum productivity, and longer sessions are more productive. Different writers find that different times of day and different locations are more conducive to productivity and creativity.

Tracking your output each day can make you more aware of your productivity and spur you to improve and adjust your tactics. Just as you clock in and out at an hourly job, create a document or worksheet where you note the date, location, starting time, ending time, ending word count, and any unusual factors (major interruptions, etc.) for each session. At the end of each week, review the information to identify the factors that helped and those that hindered. While you may not be able to change when and where you have every writing session, take those factors into account whenever possible and make changes to maximize your productivity.

Where are you most productive and creative?

_____

_____

_____

What is it about each location that makes you more or less productive and creative?

_____

_____

_____

What distractions tend to interrupt your writing or prevent you from writing?

_____

_____

_____

What is your productivity (words per hour) for each length of session (one hour, 90 minutes, etc.)?

_____

What time of day are you most productive?

_____

Treat your writing appointments as some of the most important time on your calendar each week. Show up on time and quickly get to work.

Use the first few minutes of each writing session to review who you are writing for (your target market), how your book will help them, where you are in your plan, and what you need to accomplish next. As you write, add any new questions or ideas to the plan rather than chasing those rabbits when you are in writing mode. Having a place to capture questions and ideas also helps you avoid forgetting them while you are trying to focus on writing something else.

Use the last few minutes of each session to review what you have accomplished and to plan what you will accomplish next just as a hiker on the Appalachian Trail refers to their map and GPS navigator regularly to figure out where they are, confirm where they are going, and make sure they are headed in the right direction. If you've identified new questions then schedule a research appointment to answer them.

Some writers find they can increase their productivity by using some version of the Pomodoro Technique where a short break is taken every 25 minutes to allow the mind to relax, recover, and prepare for another period of activity. As with all these suggestions, test this tactic to determine what works best for you.

Just as hikers need rest and energy to perform well, so do writers. Most people burn more calories from brain activity during an average day than from any other activity. Eat well, stay hydrated, exercise, and get enough sleep so your energy level is optimum during your writing appointments.

Develop a starting ritual that accomplishes something quick and easy to build momentum. Write a quick sentence or two based on what you've been thinking about relative to your topic and your customer personas, and use those sentences to break loose from any inertia and to get writing at full speed.

Many writers find that attempting to edit while writing substantially reduces their output. Productivity may suffer due to the brain's inability to write creatively and edit critically at the same time or the brain's inability to quickly switch back and forth between writing and editing. Regardless of the cause, many authors find they are much more productive when they focus on writing until the first draft is complete. Once the first draft is complete, then they can schedule editing appointments to focus on the second draft.

During your writing appointments, follow your plan as you allow the writing to flow in a stream of consciousness onto the paper or screen. You've done your research and the ideas have been germinating in your subconscious mind. Now you can experience the exhilaration of having them erupt into your first draft. Don't worry about spelling, grammar, syntax, or structure—capture your thoughts and ideas as quickly as possible as you elaborate on what you have outlined in your plan. You will have plenty of time for editing after you finish your first draft. Enjoy the opportunity to just write—even the opportunity to see what mistakes your mind naturally makes if you just let it be creative.

As your productivity increases, allow yourself to experience the joy of writing faster. Doing so can increase your productivity even more. Most writers also find their productivity peaks and their ability to focus and ignore distractions seems to improve when they are writing content that interests them the most and that they have been looking forward to writing. So get excited about what you have the opportunity to focus on and about the impact each paragraph could have on your readers.

Write with your customer personas in mind: What do they need to read? Imagine them gathered around you again and that they have helped you develop your plan. They need to know what you know about the topic—they need your help. Start at the beginning and write what you would tell them. Use a conversational style with short, simple sentences. What questions would they ask? What questions would they not know to ask? Write enough to answer them, provide any additional information they need to know, and then move on to discuss another subtopic. Whenever appropriate, emphasize practical action steps the reader can take to solve their problem or move closer to their goal.

Avoid unproductive rabbit trails including checking the news or social media sites or doing anything else other than writing—you have plenty of other time for those pursuits. Do not spend writing time researching or reviewing research—again, you have plenty of other time for those pursuits. Add any new ideas or items to research to the plan for your book and schedule research appointments only as necessary to answer those urgent questions. Each writing appointment you have scheduled is the time for producing words that form sentences that form paragraphs that form chapters that form books.

If you get bogged down or stuck then try putting yourself in your customer's chair and working backwards. What do they need to read? What is going to be most helpful and enjoyable to them? What are they dealing with that caused them to buy your book? What concepts will help them understand and deal with the issue at hand?

Getting bogged down or stuck is usually a good indication you are uncertain about that particular subtopic in your plan. Write what you can and then quickly make a note in your plan describing what remains unwritten and schedule a research appointment so you can work through any questions or uncertainty at another time. Then move on to the next part in your plan to get back up to speed.

As you write your manuscript, capture attribution information in footnotes, endnotes, or a bibliography to identify your sources and properly cite any quotes or other third party content. If you want to use a quote of roughly 100 words or more or to quote any song lyrics or poetry or from any other relatively short body of work then you must obtain formal permission and perhaps even pay for it.

To do so, identify the publisher of the work that contains the content you want to quote and search for "permission request form <publisher>" to obtain that publisher's form. It is important to use the correct form as the information required varies between publishers' forms. Some publishers have you complete an online form while others have you download a file that you fill in and return according to the instructions on the form. Obtaining permissions is an important part of your work as an author and can take months. If using the quote is not clearly "fair use" and you can't obtain permission then do not quote the material. You may paraphrase or summarize it and must still give proper attribution.

In addition, capture ideas for additional features and their benefits on the plan for your book. Offer features that add value to the book, distinguish it from the competition, and drive your readers to your blog and Facebook Page where you can interact with them and capture their contact information so you can market future books to them directly.

Building your audience and customer base greatly reduces the cost and time required to market new books. Your ability to drive sales and develop a snowball effect using word-of-mouth promotion can increase your likelihood of appearing on bestseller lists or generate more personal income depending on whether you direct your audience to buy from retailers or directly from you.

Such features can include videos, podcast episodes, or blog posts that allow you to provide updated or additional information on your topic and maintain the reader's interest between books. Other possible features include a monthly webinar during the year after your book releases, a study guide to facilitate group discussion, an assessment to help the reader determine how the material applies to them, special edition autographed copies of your book, forms or templates your readers need, or anything else your readers would find valuable. Announce each of these features when relevant in the chapters of your book and summarize them on a page of your site (as we have done at www.PeteNikolai.com/writeyourbook) that you point readers to again in the afterword or final chapter of your book.

You now know what it is going to take to finish your first draft:

—— unplug your television and put it in the closet or attic

—— develop your proposal

—— develop your writing plan

—— schedule limited appointments for platform development, author education, and research and abundant appointments for writing

—— put this book and all other distractions away, honor your writing appointments, use your writing plan, enjoy being a writer, and come back to this book only when you have finished your first draft

STEP 6 \ EDITING YOUR SECOND DRAFT

Congratulations! If you are reading this then you should have completed your first draft. If not then put this book and all other distractions away, honor your writing appointments, use your writing plan, enjoy being a writer, and come back to this book only when you have finished your first draft.

Finishing a first draft is the hardest step for most aspiring authors, so you should be more than two thirds of the way to finishing your book. Next up is editing. You have quickly written a mass of words as you let your thoughts and ideas flow. Your creative mind has provided you with some amazing content to work with along with an abundance of spelling, grammar, syntax, and structural errors and issues. Your critical mind can now take over to organize and clean things up.

The amount of time necessary for editing will vary, but use two hours for every thousand words you have written as a rough estimate. Just as you were able to estimate when you could finish writing your first draft, you can also estimate when you could be finished editing your second draft. Divide the number of words you have written (found in the bottom left corner of the screen if you are using Microsoft Word) by a thousand, round the result up to the next whole number, and multiply that whole number by two to estimate the number of editing hours. Replace each of the writing appointments coming up with editing appointments until you have scheduled all the editing time and then add a "celebrate finishing second draft" appointment on the next Friday or Saturday.

As we said in the first chapter: If you need to know how to quickly write a high quality nonfiction book that provides helpful information to your readers, then this book is for you. Far too many writers have manuscripts they just can't bring themselves to consider finished because they are not perfect. Your goal is to finish a book that provides helpful information to readers, not to impress them with your ability to produce a perfect book. It's not about you; it's about helping your readers.

As with writing, edit with your customer personas in mind. Imagine them gathered around you yet once again. They need to know what you know about the topic—they need your help. Start at the beginning and work through what you have written. In addition to fixing any spelling, grammar, syntax, and structural errors and issues, confirm each sentence is short, simple, and written in a conversational style. Have you written enough to answer their questions but not so much that the content begins to sound redundant? Have you emphasized practical action steps the reader can take to solve their problem? Do those steps flow in a logical progression to move the reader closer to their goal?

You now know what it is going to take to finish your second draft:

— keep your television unplugged and in the closet or attic

— confirm you have limited appointments scheduled for platform development, author education, and research and abundant appointments scheduled for editing

— put this book and all other distractions away, honor your editing appointments, enjoy being a writer, and come back to this book only when you have finished editing your second draft

STEP 7 > COLLABORATING ON YOUR FINAL READ-THROUGH

Congratulations! If you are reading this then you should have completed your second draft. If not then put this book and all other distractions away, honor your editing appointments, enjoy being a writer, and come back to this book only when you have finished editing your second draft.

Finishing the second draft can be the most tedious step for most aspiring authors, so you should be more than 90% of the way to finishing your book. Next up is a final read-through and edit. You have a manuscript with very few spelling, grammar, syntax, and structural errors and issues. It provides helpful information to your readers, flows logically in a conversational style, and contains practical action steps the reader can take to solve their problem. Your critical mind can now finish the job with the help of a friend.

You need another person because they bring a fresh perspective, and you will be blind to any remaining errors by the time you finish your second draft. The person should be somebody you trust to be brutally honest when they identify something that should be fixed. They should understand English (somebody who majored in English or a related field would be best) and preferably be representative of your target market. You will need to be receptive to their opinion and have an attitude of thankfulness for their help in making your manuscript better.

The amount of time necessary for the read-through will vary, but use 15 minutes for every thousand words you have written as a rough estimate. Just as you were able to estimate when you could finish writing your first draft and editing your second draft, you can also estimate when you could be finished with your read-through—and your book! Divide the number of words you have written (found in the bottom left corner of the screen if you are using Microsoft Word) by a thousand, round the result up to the next whole number, and multiply that whole number by 15 to estimate the number of minutes for your read-through. Contact your friend to schedule an appointment or two to allow for all the time necessary—plus an additional 30 minutes to celebrate finishing your book!

At the start of your appointment, explain to your friend that you will be working together to do the final read-through with your customer personas in mind so they are to try to provide feedback from your target market's perspective. Also explain that you will read through the entire book in the time you have scheduled and will use any remaining time to quickly read through parts of it again.

Start at the beginning and take turns reading through your manuscript out loud and discussing any issues that should be addressed. In addition to fixing any spelling, grammar, syntax, and structural errors and issues, confirm each sentence is short, simple, and written in a conversational style. Have you written enough to answer your customers' questions but not so much that the content begins to sound redundant? Have you emphasized practical action steps the reader can take to solve their problem? Do those steps flow in a logical progression to move the reader closer to their goal?

You now know what it is going to take to do your final read-through and finish your book:

— select an appropriate friend to help you

— schedule the necessary appointments

— do your final read-through with your friend and celebrate finishing your book!

PART THREE

WHAT'S NEXT?

C ongratulations! If you are reading this then you should have completed your final read-through and your book. If not then put this book and all other distractions away, schedule and keep the necessary appointments with a friend, enjoy being a writer, and come back to this book only when you have finished your final read-through.

Again, congratulations on finishing your book! You now have a manuscript that is ready for the publishing process.

So what's next? How do you intend to get your manuscript published?

Technology is changing the way authors publish their books by removing the gatekeepers and intermediaries or at least transferring more of the control and benefits to the authors. While this creates new expectations that can be frustrating for traditional authors, agents, publishers, and bookstores, it opens up the process for many new participants by removing some of the barriers to entry.

In the past few years, as more self-published titles have made their way on to bestseller lists and several successful authors have chosen to self-publish, the "vanity" stigma that was previously attached to self-publishing has been replaced by reluctant acceptance by many in the industry. Some are even embracing self-publishing and realizing that authors who successfully self-publish believe in themselves enough to invest in their book and have proven themselves capable of driving sales—things every competent publisher wants in an author.

Authors now have at least five options when publishing their books:

1. Traditional Publishing: the author contracts with an agent to try to get their book acquired by a traditional publisher in hopes that the author will receive a large royalty advance up front and can outsource most of the tasks after writing (and sometimes even the writing)

2. Hybrid Self-Publishing: the author contracts with a hybrid publisher (a traditional publisher that provides self-publishing services in order to monitor the performance of those titles with an eye toward acquiring those that are successful) to have them manage most of the various tasks involved in publishing and marketing the book

3. Assisted Self-Publishing: the author contracts with a self-publishing services provider to have them manage most of the various tasks involved in publishing and marketing the book

4. Managed Self-Publishing: the author serves as their own project manager to contract with and manage the people needed to complete the various tasks involved in publishing and marketing the book

5. Do-It-Yourself (DIY) Self-Publishing: the author publishes the book by doing each of the various tasks involved in publishing and marketing the book (very few people have the skills, knowledge, and experience required—and

those who do usually come to the conclusion that their time is better invested in the tasks that provide the highest return and the most enjoyment)

As the author of a finished manuscript, you have a variety of options available as you consider how to get your book published. We are in the process of writing *Publish Your Book* to provide the information you need and to explain the various processes. If you subscribe to our blog at www.PeteNikolai.com then you will be notified when it is available.

AFTERWORD

Thank you for allowing us to guide you through the process of writing and finishing your book!

If you have any feedback on this book then feel free to leave a comment at www.PeteNikolai.com/writeyourbook

On that web page you will find any updated information as well as the forms mentioned in this book and a convenient list of the various links. You can also share any thoughts you may have on becoming more successful as a writer in the comments section on that page.

If you found this book helpful then please recommend it to other writers and review it on the website for the store where you bought it and on one of the major sites for reading such as GoodReads, Shelfari, or LibraryThing.

The royalties earned on this book in 2014 and 2015 are being paid directly to Reading Is Fundamental (RIF), the largest children's literacy nonprofit in the United States. If you are looking for a way to use your writing to help others then please consider having your royalties paid to RIF too. If you do so then please visit www.brighthopefortomorrow.org for information on how to use free "cause marketing" to promote your title to drive more sales and generate more royalties to support literacy.

ACCOMPLISHING YOUR GOALS AND LIVING ON PURPOSE

Questions were provided throughout this book to help you capture your perspective on some important issues. Now is the time to go back, review, and finish answering each of those questions as you lay the foundation for pursuing your vision and achieving your goals.

Once you have finished answering each question, take some time to revisit each of them to see where you stand. Add a projected completion date to each goal if you have not done so already to help establish your commitment, provide perspective, and initiate action.

Use the following four-step process to accomplish your goals:

1. Review your goals and note the Top Three. You determine the criteria for what makes a goal one of your Top Three—they are your goals. You might choose those that are the most urgent or important, or you might

pick three you can complete quickly. Each should start with a verb (create, write, etc.), be measurable (so you know when you have completed it), and have a projected completion date. Add each goal to your calendar on its projected completion date.

What are your Top Three Goals?

_____

_____

_____

2. Make sure you have listed the complete sequence of action steps for each goal that will take you from where you are to accomplishing that goal. If you find there is no clear set of action steps to take to accomplish a particular goal because some of the steps are out of your control or even unknown, then acknowledge you've identified a difficult goal. Add it to a separate list of Difficult Goals and replace it on your Top Three list. Schedule a monthly appointment to review your Difficult Goals in light of any new understanding you may have gained or any factors outside your control that may have come together to accomplish something you could not.

3. Review your Top Three Goals list (with action steps) each day and complete as many action steps as possible. Each step you take, no matter how small, takes you a step closer to accomplishing that goal and seeing your vision become reality. It is the little steps taken each day that separate the successful from those with good intentions.

4. When you have completed a Top Three Goal then celebrate with a friend, help them establish their Top Three, and then review your other options and add a new goal to your Top Three (don't forget to add the new goal to your calendar on its projected completion date).

Schedule a recurring appointment to refer back to your purpose, vision, and goals regularly so you remain focused and headed in the direction you have chosen and have the opportunity to change course if doing so becomes necessary. Reminding yourself of your goals and believing they are important to you and to those you are trying to impact provides the motivation to take the next action step and helps develop an attitude that makes perseverance possible. Neglecting to remember (aka forgetting) why your goals are important can lead to procrastination and delays.

We tend to be motivated by things that pay off quickly or allow us to avoid pain of some kind. Focusing on goals that may not be accomplished for months, if ever, requires a level of willpower few seem to possess. It is far too easy to deal with the seemingly urgent matters of the day while the important stuff gathers dust.

And in that problem lies the solution: Find a way to make the important stuff urgent by building in short term rewards along the way and pain of some kind if you neglect to take action. One easy way to do this is to announce your Top Three Goals and your next action steps (such as writing a specified number of words in the next week) on Facebook or to a few close friends. Let your friends know you will report your progress every Sunday evening, and ask them to hold you accountable by simply agreeing to receive a short weekly Top Three Goals email update from you and to reply with a word or two of encouragement when you are making progress and appropriate comments when you are not. Then schedule a recurring appointment to send that weekly email. We care what people think of us so our performance will usually improve dramatically.

Following these steps will cause you to be intentional in pursuing your vision, accomplishing your goals, and living on purpose.

GHOSTWRITING AND OTHER FORMS OF COLLABORATION

Many books are written using a collaborative process often referred to as ghostwriting where the author comes up with the idea and provides some of the information but another writer writes the manuscript. An author will hire a writer when they realize they will not have the time necessary to write their book on schedule or that they are gifted in areas other than writing and need a writer to create a book worth reading. Some authors choose to collaborate to increase their output or to benefit from additional expertise on the subject matter.

The ethical question of whether to acknowledge each collaborator on the front cover or in the front matter of the book has been debated for years. If you decide to collaborate on a book then establish a written agreement in advance that includes provisions describing the credit each person will receive. As when hiring any service professional, obtain referrals and discuss the writer's performance with those referrals.

If you are considering whether to have somebody help you write your book, it may be helpful to consider how much you would have to pay somebody to generate the results you want and then compare that amount with the value you could generate if you choose to use that time to focus on your most valuable work rather than writing. For example, if you can generate $40 per hour by selling more of a product or service and you can hire a writer for $20 per hour to do a better job writing your book than you can then it makes sense to hire a writer so you can keep selling. However if you are making $10 per hour at a second job and can write as quickly and as well as a writer you can hire for $20 per hour then it makes sense to work fewer hours and use that time to write your book yourself rather than paying the writer to write it.

BIBLIOGRAPHY

Source materials listed are not necessarily recommended but were used in the research for this book. This bibliography is also available at www.PeteNikolai.com/writeyourbook with a link to each item for your convenience.

Aaron, Rachel. *2,000 to 10,000: Writing Faster, Writing Better, and Writing More of What You Love.* 2012.

American Psychological Association. *Publication Manual of the American Psychological Association*, 6th ed. 2009.

Amir, Nina. *How to Blog a Book: Write, Publish, and Promote Your Work One Post at a Time.* 2012.

Asselin, Barb. *Write a Kindle Bestseller: How to Write, Format, Publish, and Market a Kindle Bestseller.* 2014.

Atchity, Kenneth. *Write Time: Guide to the Creative Process, from Vision through Revision and Beyond*, 3d ed (previously titled *A Writer's Time*). 2011.

Ballenger, Bruce. *The Curious Researcher: A Guide to Writing Research Papers*, 7th ed. 2011.

Belcher, Wendy Laura. *Writing Your Journal Article in Twelve Weeks: A Guide to Academic Publishing Success.* 2009.

Bloomberg, Linda Dale, and Marie F. Volpe. *Completing Your Qualitative Dissertation: A Road Map from Beginning to End*, 2d ed. 2012.

Boice, Robert. *Professors as Writers: A Self-Help Guide to Productive Writing.* 1990.

Booth, Wayne C., Gregory G. Colomb, and, Joseph M. Williams. *The Craft of Research*, 3d ed. 2008.

Bowerman, Peter. *The Well-Fed Writer: Financial Self-Sufficiency as a Commercial Freelancer in Six Months or Less*, 2d ed. 2009.

Brande, Dorothea. *Becoming a Writer.* 1934. Reprint, with a foreword by John Gardner, 1981.

Burns, Nathaniel. *How I Make $4,000 a Month Selling Ebooks on Amazon Kindle and How You Can Too.* 2014.

Cameron, Julia. *The Artist's Way*, 2d ed. 2002.

Casagrande, June. *It Was the Best of Sentences, It Was the Worst of Sentences: A Writer's Guide to Crafting Killer Sentences.* 2010.

Clark, Roy Peter. *Writing Tools: 50 Essential Strategies for Every Writer.* 2006.

Corson-Knowles, Tom. *Secrets of the Six Figure Author: Mastering the Inner Game of Writing, Publishing, and Marketing Books.* 2013.

Corson-Knowles, Tom. *The Kindle Writing Bible: How to Write a Bestselling Nonfiction Book from Start to Finish*. 2013.

Denney, Jim. *Write Fearlessly!* 2013

Denney, Jim. *Writing in Overdrive: Write Faster, Write Freely, Write Brilliantly*. 2013.

Eckstein, Kristen. *Author's Quick Guide to Creating a Killer Non-Fiction Book Title*. 2013.

Eckstut, Arielle, and David Henry Sterry. *The Essential Guide to Getting Your Book Published: How to Write It, Sell It, and Market It… Successfully!* 2010.

Fogarty, Mignon. *Grammar Girl's Quick and Dirty Tips for Better Writing*. 2008.

Foss, Sonja K., and William Waters. *Destination Dissertation: A Traveler's Guide to a Done Dissertation*. 2007.

Foster, Alex. *Writing a Kindle Book a Week*. 2013.

Foster, Jack. *How to Get Ideas*, 2d ed. 2007.

Garner, Bryan A. *Garner's Modern American Usage*, 3d ed. 2009.

Goodson, Patricia. *Becoming an Academic Writer: 50 Exercises for Paced, Productive, and Powerful Writing*. 2012.

Graff, Gerald, and Cathy Birkenstein. *They Say, I Say: The Moves that Matter in Academic Writing with Readings*, 2d ed. 2012.

Gutkind, Lee. *You Can't Make This Stuff Up: The Complete Guide to Writing Creative Nonfiction from Memoir to Literary Journalism and Everything in Between*. 2012.

Hacker, Diana, and Nancy Sommers. *A Pocket Style Manual*, 6th ed. 2011.

Hacker, Diana, and Nancy Sommers. *A Writer's Reference*, 7th ed. 2010.

Hacker, Diana, and Nancy Sommers. *Rules for Writers*, 7th ed. 2011.

Hale, Constance. *Sin and Syntax: How to Craft Wickedly Effective Prose*. 1999.

Hall, James W. *Hit Lit: Cracking the Code of the Twentieth Century's Biggest Bestsellers*. 2012.

Hart, Jack. *A Writer's Coach: An Editor's Guide to Words That Work*. 2006.

Hart, Jack. *Storycraft: The Complete Guide to Writing Narrative Nonfiction*. 2011.

Heath, Terry. *Write an eBook in 14 Days*. 2013.

Hendrickson, Nancy L. *How to Write for Kindle: A Non-Fiction Book in 72 Hours or Less*. 2013.

Hufford, Bryan. *Write Fast: 21 Powerful Ways to Cut Your Writing Time in Half*. 2013.

Hyatt, Michael S. *Everything You Need to Know to Get Published!* 2012. MP3. http://www.learnhowtogetpublished.com (accessed March 5, 2014).

Hyatt, Michael S. *Writing a Winning Non-Fiction Book Proposal.* 2009.

Johnston, Marcia Riefer. *Word Up! How to Write Powerful Sentences and Paragraphs (And Everything You Build from Them).* 2013.

Junttila, Henri. *How to Write Nonfiction eBooks: A Proven 17-Step Plan for Beginners.* 2014.

Kawasaki, Guy, and Shawn Welch. *APE: Author, Publisher, Entrepreneur,* 2d ed. 2013.

Kaye, Sanford. *Writing Under Pressure: The Quick Writing Process.* 1990.

Kennedy, Marcy. *How to Write Faster.* 2013.

Kidder, Tracy, and Richard Todd. *Good Prose: The Art of Nonfiction.* 2013.

King, Stephen. *On Writing: A Memoir of the Craft,* 10th anniversary ed. 1999.

Kleon, Austin. *Steal Like an Artist: 10 Things Nobody Told You About Being Creative.* 2012.

Kozik, Donna. *Write a Book in a Weekend: 7 "Insider" Author Strategies.* 2009.

Lamott, Anne. *Bird by Bird: Some Instructions on Writing and Life.* 1995.

LaRocque, Paula. *The Book on Writing: The Ultimate Guide to Writing Well.* 2003.

Larsen, Michael. *How to Write a Book Proposal,* 4th ed. 2011.

Leedy, Paul D., and Jeanne Ellis Ormrod. *Practical Research: Planning and Design,* 10th ed. 2012.

Lester, James D., and James D. Lester Jr. *Writing Research Papers: A Complete Guide,* 14th ed. 2011.

Lott, Bret. *Letters and Life: On Being a Writer, On Being a Christian.* 2013.

Lukeman, Noah. *The First Five Pages: A Writer's Guide to Staying Out of the Rejection Pile.* 2000.

McCloskey, Deirdre. *Economical Writing,* 2d ed. 1999.

McIndoo, Ann. *7 Easy Steps to Write Your Book: How to Get Your Book Out of Your Head and a Manuscript in Your Hands!* 2011.

McKenna, Bridget. *The Little Book of Self-Editing for Writers: 12 Ways to Take Your Book from Good to Great.* 2012.

McMullen, Chris. *How to Self-Publish a Book on Amazon.com: Writing, Editing, Designing, Publishing, and Marketing.* 2009.

Messick, Mark LeGrand. *How to Write a Nonfiction Ebook in 24 Days.* 2014.

Modern Language Association. *MLA Handbook for Writers of Research Papers,* 7th ed. 2009.

Nicholson, Scott. *The Indie Journey: Secrets to Writing Success.* 2011.

Nicholson, Scott, ed. *Write Good or Die: Survival Tips for the 21st Century.* 2010.

Patterson, Kerry, Joseph Grenny, Ron McMillan, and Al Switzler. *Crucial Conversations: Tools for Talking When Stakes Are High.* 2002

Perrin, Robert. *Pocket Guide to APA Style,* 5th ed. 2014.

Platt, Sean, and Johnny B. Truant with David Wright. *Write. Publish. Repeat.* 2014.

Platt, Sean. *Writing Online: Write Your Dreams to Reality.* 2011.

Pressfield, Steven. *Do the Work.* 2011.

Pressfield, Steven. *The War of Art: Winning the Inner Creative Battle.* 2002.

Pressfield, Steven. *Turning Pro: Tap Your Inner Power and Create Your Life's Work.* 2012.

Pyne, Stephen J. *Voice and Vision: A Guide to Writing History and Other Serious Nonfiction.* 2009.

Rabiner, Susan, and Alfred Fortunato. *Thinking Like Your Editor: How to Write Great Serious Nonfiction--and Get it Published.* 2002.

Roman, Kenneth, and Joel Raphaelson. *Writing That Works: How to Communicate Effectively in Business*, 3d ed. 2010.

Rudestam, Kjell Erik, and Rae R. Newton. *Surviving Your Dissertation: A Comprehensive Guide to Content and Process*, 3d ed. 2007.

Scott, S. J. *Writing Habit Mastery: How to Write 2,000 Words a Day and Forever Cure Writer's Block.* 2013.

Scott, Steve. *How to Discover Best-Selling Nonfiction eBook Ideas: The Bulletproof Strategy.* 2012

Scott, Steve. *How to Write a Nonfiction eBook in 21 Days that Readers Love!* 2012.

Shapiro, Dani. *Still Writing: The Perils and Pleasures of a Creative Life.* 2013

Silvia, Paul J. *How to Write a Lot: A Practical Guide to Productive Academic Writing.* 2007.

Skillin, Marjorie E., and Robert M. Gay. *Words into Type*, 3d ed. 1974.

Smith, Marion Roach. *The Memoir Project: A Thoroughly Non-Standardized Text for Writing and Life*, 2d ed (previously titled *Writing What You Know: Realia*). 2011.

Stables, Ian. *Questions that Easily Write Books: How to Write a Nonfiction Ebook Using a Simple Outline Method.* 2012.

Strunk, William, Jr., and E. B. White. *The Elements of Style,* 4th ed. 1999.

Sword, Helen. *Stylish Academic Writing.* 2012.

Tharp, Twyla. *The Creative Habit: Learn It and Use It for Life.* 2003.

Thurman, Susan. *The Only Grammar Book You'll Ever Need.* 2003.

Truss, Lynne. *Eats, Shoots and Leaves: The Zero Tolerance Approach to Punctuation.* 2004.

Turabian, Kate L., Wayne C. Booth, Gregory G. Colomb, Joseph M. Williams, and University of Chicago Press Staff. *A Manual for Writers of Research Papers, Theses, and Dissertations: Chicago Style for Students and Researchers,* 8th ed. 2013.

Ueland, Brenda. *If You Want to Write: A Book about Art, Independence, and Spirit.* 1938. Reprint 2007.

University of Chicago Press Staff. *The Chicago Manual of Style,* 16th ed. 2010.

Wendig, Chuck. *250 Things You Should Know About Writing.* 2011.

Weston, Anthony. *A Rulebook for Arguments,* 4th ed. 2008.

Wilson, Douglas. *Wordsmithy: Hot Tips for the Writing Life.* 2011.

Yardley, Cathy. *Write Every Day: How to Write Faster, and Write More.* 2013.

Zinsser, William. *On Writing Well: The Classic Guide to Writing Nonfiction*, 30th anniversary ed. 2006.

Zinsser, William. *Writing about Your Life: A Journey into the Past.* 2004.

ABOUT THE AUTHORS

PETE NIKOLAI has been in the book publishing business since 1991, working in a variety of roles including sales, product development, and management for Thomas Nelson Publishers (a division of HarperCollins Christian Publishing). He is the Director of Publishing Services for HarperCollins Christian Publishing and Publisher of WestBow Press which he has managed since overseeing its launch in 2009.

AMELIA NIKOLAI manages the day-to-day operations of the couple's writing business and the nonprofit they have started, Bright Hope for Tomorrow, which helps authors use "cause marketing" to drive sales and support literacy and math education. She uses her background in design and project management to add planning and action to Pete's ideas and intentions.

Amelia and Pete live in Nashville and enjoy a variety of activities together including reading, travelling, and volunteering. They blog at www.PeteNikolai.com and speak at writers conferences and other events.